Quotable Earth

summersdale

QUOTABLE EARTH

Summersdale Publishers Ltd
46 West Street
Chichester
West Sussex
PO19 1RP
UK

www.summersdale.com

Printed and bound in Singapore

All images © Shutterstock

ISBN: 978-1-84024-748-0

Substantial discounts on bulk quantities of Summersdale books are available to corporations, professional associations and other organisations. For details telephone Summersdale Publishers on (+44-1243-771107), fax (+44-1243-786300) or email (nicky@summersdale.com).

Quotable Earth

In every out thrust headland, in every curving **beach**, in every grain of **sand** there is a story of the **earth**.

Rachel Carson

On **earth** there is no **heaven,**
but there are **pieces of it.**

Jules Renard

To sit in the shade on a **fine day** and look upon verdure is the most perfect **refreshment**.

Jane Austen

One **touch of nature** makes the whole world **kin**.

William Shakespeare

In **all things** of nature there is something of the **marvellous**.

Aristotle

Nature is an **infinite** sphere of which the centre is **everywhere** and the circumference nowhere.

Blaise Pascal

Pleasure is spread through the earth in **stray gifts** to be claimed by whoever shall **find.**

William Wordsworth

Study nature, love nature, stay close to **nature**. It will never fail you.

Frank Lloyd Wright

What makes the **desert**
beautiful is that somewhere it
hides a well.

Antoine de Saint-Exupéry

The **poetry** of the earth is **never dead.**

John Keats

Give me a spark of **nature's fire**. That's all the **learning** I desire.

Robert Burns

The **goal of life** is living in **agreement** with nature.

Zeno

Trees are the earth's endless effort to **speak** to the listening **heaven**.

Rabindranath Tagore

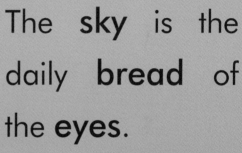

The **sky** is the
daily **bread** of
the **eyes**.

Ralph Waldo Emerson

To **forget** how to dig the **earth** and to tend the **soil** is to forget ourselves.

Mohandas K. Gandhi

There is no **excellent beauty** that hath not some **strangeness** in the proportion.

Francis Bacon

Nature is full of **genius**, full of the **divinity**; so that not a **snowflake** escapes its fashioning hand.

Henry David Thoreau

Earth is here so **kind**, that just **tickle** her with a hoe and she laughs with a **harvest**.

Douglas Jerrold

I'd rather have **roses** on my table than **diamonds** on my neck.

Emma Goldman

Look **deep** into nature, and then you will **understand** everything better.

Albert Einstein

Nothing is more beautiful than the **loveliness** of the **woods** before **sunrise.**

George Washington Carver

If you truly **love nature**, you will find beauty everywhere.

Vincent Van Gogh

In the **hope** of reaching the moon
men fail to see the **flowers that**
blossom at their feet.

Albert Schweitzer

Those who dwell among the **beauties** and mysteries of the earth are **never alone** or weary of life.

Rachel Carson

One sees **great things** from the **valley**, only small things from the **peak**.

G. K. Chesterton

The **sun** does not **shine** for a few trees and flowers, but for the **wide world's joy**.

Henry Ward Beecher

What is a weed? A plant whose **virtues** have not yet been discovered.

Ralph Waldo Emerson

To see a world in a **grain of sand**,
And a **heaven** in a wild flower,
Hold infinity in the palm of your hand,
An **eternity** in an hour.

William Blake

After a **thundershower**, the weather takes a pledge and signs it with a **rainbow**.

Thomas Bailey Aldrich

Each season has its **joys to treasure**, to lift one's spirits and bring us **pleasure**.

Chinese proverb

I often think that the **night** is more alive and more **richly coloured** than the day.

Vincent Van Gogh

Flowers and **butterflies** drift in colour, **illuminating** spring.

Anonymous

The **powers** of water are **immeasurable**. In the form of **ice**, it can chisel **rock** as effectively as steel.

Peggy Wayburn

In **wilderness** is the **preservation** of the world.

Henry David Thoreau

Let us permit **nature** to have her **way**. She **understands** her business better than we do.

Michel de Montaigne

The **richness** I achieve
comes from nature, the source
of **my inspiration**.

Claude Monet

Eternity begins and ends with the **ocean's tides.**

Anonymous

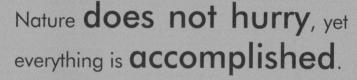

Nature **does not hurry**, yet everything is **accomplished**.

Lao Tzu

People from a planet without **flowers** would think we must be **mad with joy** the whole time to have such things **about us**.

Iris Murdoch

The real **voyage** of **discovery** consists not in seeking new **landscapes** but in having **new eyes**.

Marcel Proust

The least **movement** is of importance to all nature. The entire **ocean** is affected by a **pebble**.

Blaise Pascal

We must never lose our sense of **awe** at the **magnificence** of this **planet**.

Anonymous

How glorious a greeting the **sun** gives the mountains!

John Muir

Nature will bear the **closest inspection**. She invites us to lay our eye level with her smallest leaf, and take an **insect view** of its plain.

Henry David Thoreau

We do not **inherit** the earth from our fathers. We **borrow** it from our **children**.

David Brower

PHOTO CREDITS

Coral island © VVO
Tree and mountain © Hiroshi Ichikawa
Sunbeam wood © Claudio Beiza
Gorilla © Eric Isselée
Spider's web © Josef F. Stuefer
Niagra Falls © Gary Blakeley
Rock columns © Mario Bruno
Hummingbird © iDesign
Dunes © Kaido Kärner
Snowdrop © fotoret
Lava © juliengrondin
Humpback whale © Sandy Buckley
Tree © Pakhnyushcha
Clouds © Tyler Olson
Cracked earth © viki2win
Starfish © PBorowka
Snowflakes on glass © ELEN
Wheat field © Filipchuk Oleg Vasiliovich
Rose © Marie C. Fields
Coral fish © Specta
Autumn lake © Bruce Amos
Lightning © Martin Fischer
Bluebell wood © marilyn barbone

Wolf © Naturablichter
Mountain lake © WizData, inc.
Ocean sunset © silver-john
Dandelion © poresh
Sand prints © Elena Elisseeva
Rainbow © Olga Drozdova
Autumn forest © artjazz
Aurora borealis © Roman Krochuk
Butterfly © KSR
Iceberg © Armin Rose
Canyon © Mike Norton
Elephant swimming © DUMITRU
Lily blossom © vaklav
Breaking wave © Mana Photo
Stalactites © kavram
Sunflowers © János Gehring
Tree frog © Tom C Amon
Pebble beach © ZTS
Geyser © Videowokart
Mountain sunset © Galyna Andrushko
Red bug © Liudmila Gridina
Polar bear © Jan Martin Will

Have you enjoyed this book? If so, why not
write a review on your favourite website?

Thanks very much for buying
this Summersdale book.

www.summersdale.com